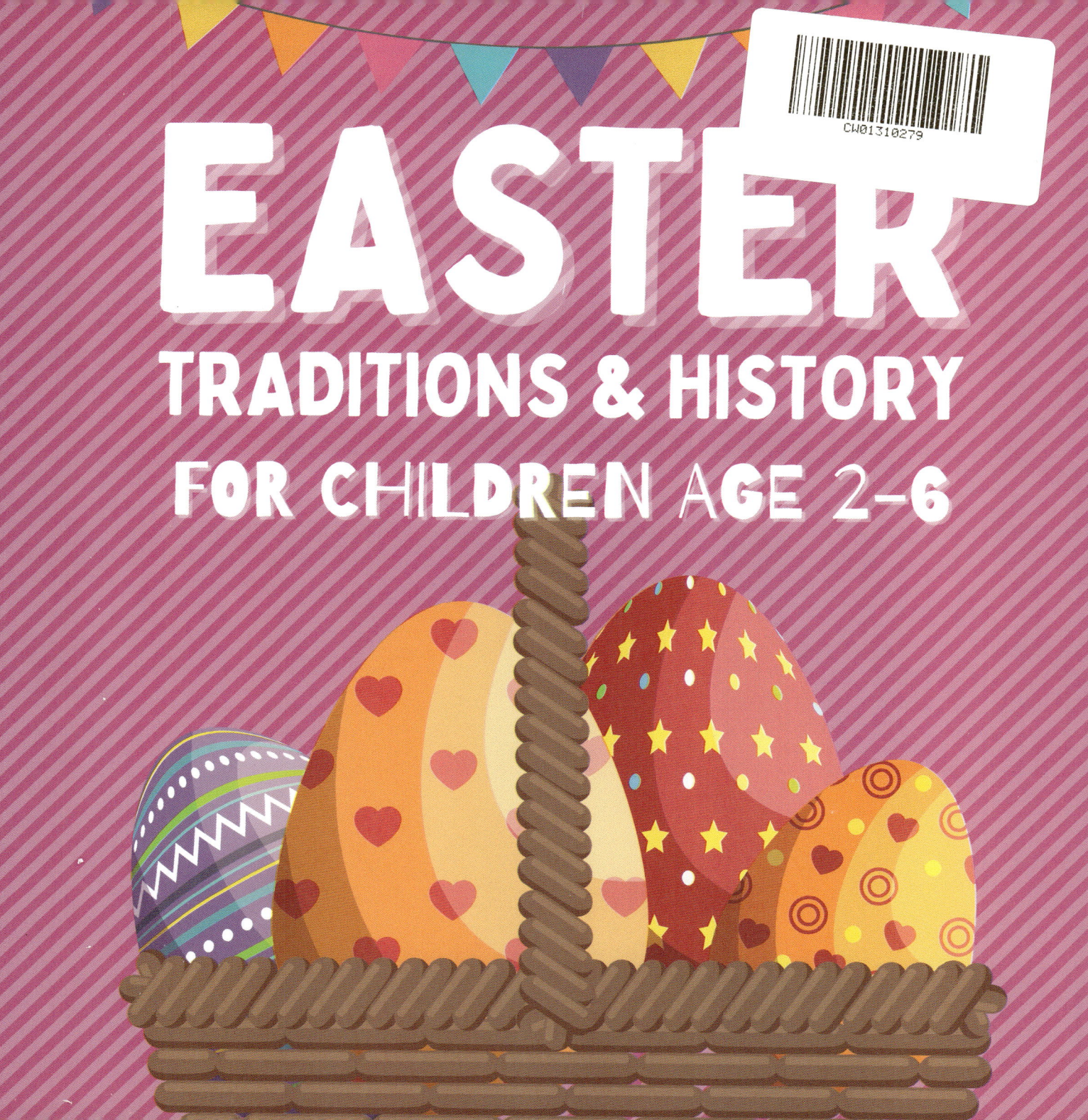
EASTER
TRADITIONS & HISTORY
FOR CHILDREN AGE 2-6

MORE KIDS BOOKS!

Farting books for kids

Luke the Leprechaun Can't Stop Farting
Louie the Leprechaun Farts for Ireland

St. Patrick's Day history & traditions for kids

Unicorn books for kids

My sister is a unicorn series
Ciara & the Unicorn's New York Adventure
Ciara & the Unicorn's Farm Fiasco
Ciara & the Unicorn's Cake Shop Surprise
Ciara & the Unicorn's Save Valentine's Day

FOR EVERY WONDERFUL CHILD WHO LOVES ALL THINGS EASTER...

THIS BOOK BELONGS TO:

What date is Easter?

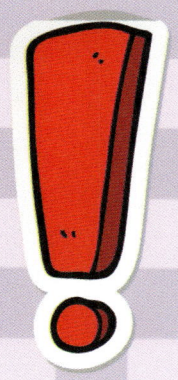 The date of Easter each year depends on the moon! Easter is on the first Sunday AFTER the Paschal full moon.

The Paschal full moon is the first full moon on or after 21 March.

Did you know? The Egg is a symbol that represents spring and new life..

On Easter Sunday, we celebrate the the history of Easter and spring, by doing fun activities with Easter Eggs!

ORGANISE AN EASTER EGG HUNT!

Hide 10 to 20 small easter eggs around your garden and invite your family or friends to find the eggs. When you find them, you can eat them!

Don't forget to decorate your house with Easter decorations!

DID YOU KNOW:

Spring is when the flowers start to grow and bloom.

Nature Activity

Pick and arrange a Spring bouquet of flowers in a vase!

Make Easter Cards for your family and friends.

All you need is some paper, some color pencils and your imagination!

How to decorate eggs for Easter!

- Ask an adult to hard boil some eggs.
- After the water starts to boil, turn off the heat. Then cover the eggs and leave them in the hot water for 15 minutes.
- Then let them cool for 20 minutes.

Now you can have fun decorating your eggs with paint, markers or chalk with your favourite colors and designs!

Stripes

Basketball

Swirls

Flowers

Dots

Hearts

Dress up in Easter costumes and have your own Easter parade.

People love parties and parades, especially at Easter!

 Where did Easter come from?

 On the Thursday before Easter, Jesus had a big dinner with 12 of his apostles. This Thursday is called 'Holy Thursday'.

Judas Iscariot was one of the Twelve Apostles at the dinner. He shared Jesus's secret location, in exchange for 30 pieces of silver. Jesus was captured.

On the Friday before Easter, Jesus died on the cross. This Friday is now called 'Good Friday'.

Later that day, Jesus met two of his friends on the road outside Emmaus. They didn't recognise him! But it was late so they asked him to stay the night with them.

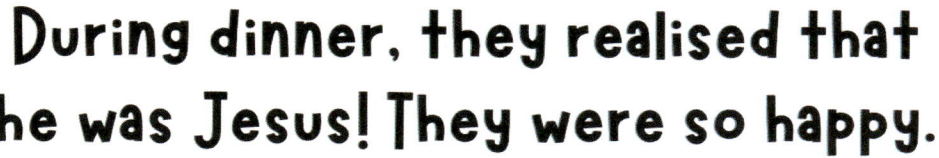

During dinner, they realised that he was Jesus! They were so happy.

The Easter Bunny is a symbol of Easter. It started in Germany and spread worldwide.

The Easter Bunny has a basket filled with Easter Eggs. His job is to decide if children were naughty or nice – just like Santa Claus!

In Scotland, people have a race and roll Easter Eggs down steep hills!

In Sweden and Finland, children dress up as Easter witches and go door to door to collect sweets and chocolate!

Easter Egg Trees

In Germany, people decorate eggs and then hang them on trees, to create Easter Egg Trees!

In Bermuda, Easter is celebrated by growing the beautiful Easter lily.

Bermuda

CONGRATULATIONS!

YOU FINISHED THIS BOOK. IF YOU ENJOYED THIS BOOK, PLEASE LEAVE A REVIEW!

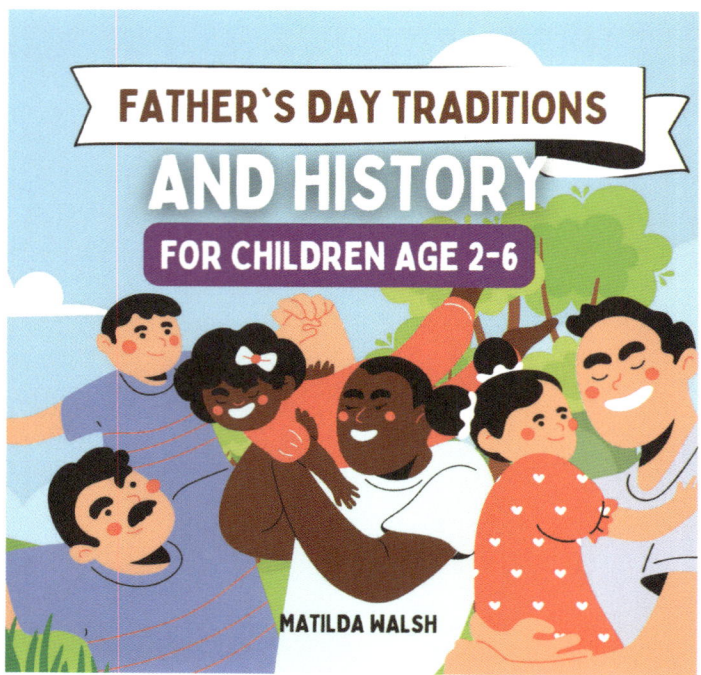

LOVE FARTS?

ENJOY THE FUNNY FARTING BOOKS!

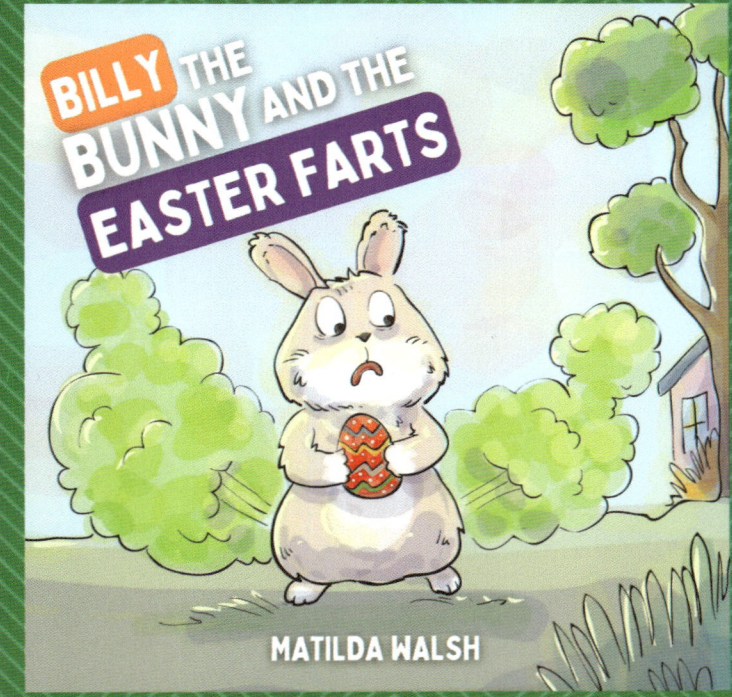

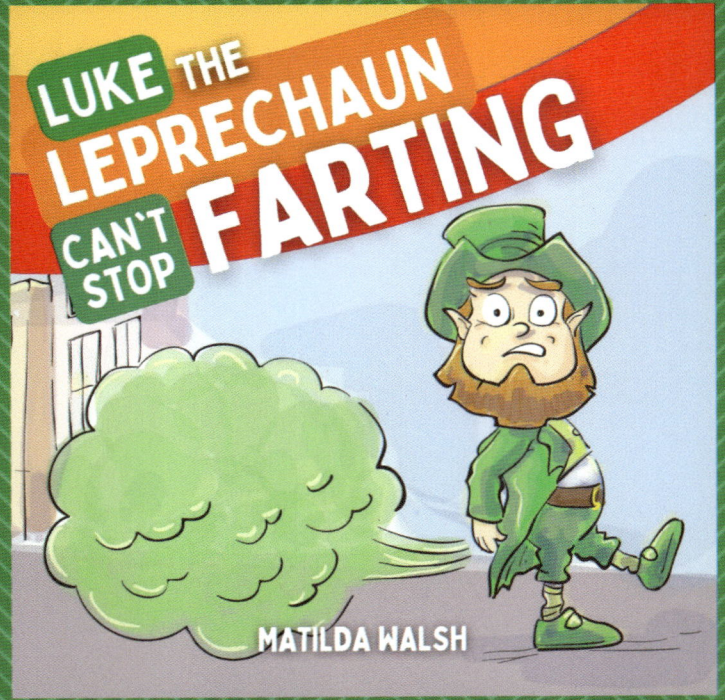

LOVE UNICORNS?

ENJOY THE FUNNY UNICORN BOOK SERIES!

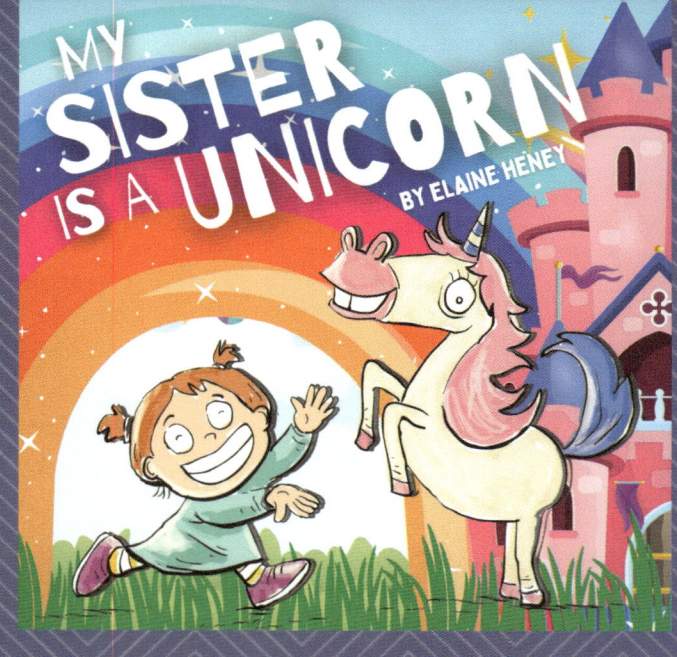

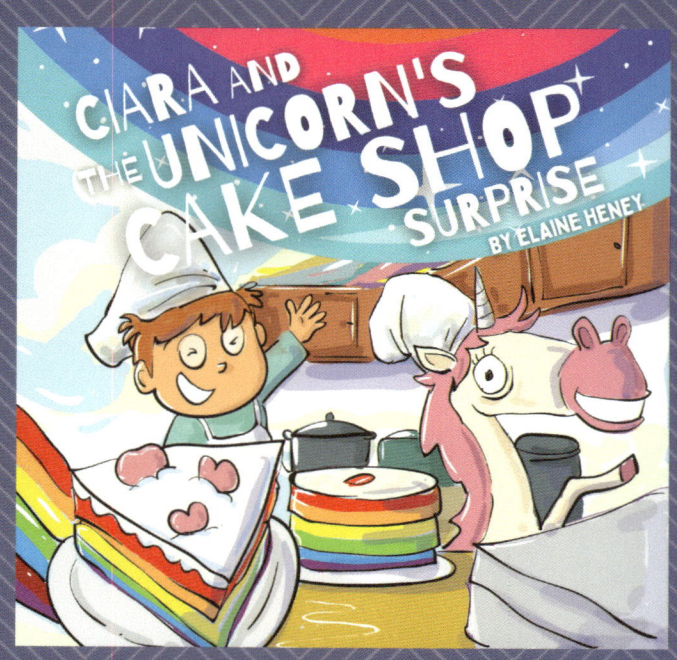

Printed in Great Britain
by Amazon